They Wish They Could Kill Me

(Figaro's Aria)

William M. Hoffman

John Corigliano

*Cue-size notes in the piano part may be used to substitute for the offstage knocking.

T0050945

JOHN CORIGLIANO

THE GHOSTS OF VERSAILLES

"They Wish They Could Kill Me"

(Figaro's Aria—Baritone)

Music by John Corigliano
Libretto by William M. Hoffman

Ed-3903
First Printing: August 1993

G. SCHIRMER, Inc.

Distributed by

Hal Leonard Publishing Corporation
7777 West Bluemound Road P.O. Box 13819 Milwaukee, WI 53213

Synopsis

The Ghosts of Versailles is set in the present in the palace of Versailles. It seems that the ghosts of the court of Louis XVI have been haunting the place since their demise during the French Revolution.

The ghost of the playwright Beaumarchais, the author of *The Barber of Seville* and *The Marriage of Figaro,* has been in love with the ghost of Marie Antoinette for the last two hundred years, but she has been so overwhelmed with grief for her thwarted life that she has ignored him.

In order to distract the queen from her misery, Beaumarchais has written an opera with the power to change history so that she does not die on the guillotine but runs off with him to the New World. He has enlisted characters from his plays, including Figaro and Susanna, and Count Almaviva and Rosina, to rescue the doomed queen.

In the opera-within-the-opera that Beaumarchais has concocted, Almaviva plans to sell the queen's necklace in order to bribe her way out of prison. The villain Bégearss, while pretending to be the count's friend and confidant, attempts to seize the jewels for himself but is stopped by the intervention of Figaro.

According to Beaumarchais' plan, Figaro was supposed to return the jewels to the count, but the valet rebels against the author's plot on the grounds that the money would be better spent rescuing his own family than the wicked queen.

The author has no recourse but to enter his own opera to force his character to obey. He convinces Figaro that the queen is worth saving by showing him the gruesome trial that condemned her to death.

In the end, Marie Antoinette is given the opportunity to escape from prison, but she refuses. She has fallen in love with the playwright and is unwilling to lose him in the after-world by altering the past. As she forgives those who took away her life, she walks off into eternity with her lover Beaumarchais.

They Wish They Could Kill Me

(Figaro's Aria)

In the prologue to his opera-with-in-the-opera, Beaumarchais introduces the wily Figaro. While he is still Count Almaviva's valet, Figaro is twenty years older than in *The Marriage of Figaro.*

He is first seen pursued by a motley group of men, women, and children—all of whom he has deceived in some way or another. He manages to elude them by seeming to hide in a closet, into which they all run after him. When they have all entered the trap, he locks the door and throws the key away. As he begins to relate the story of his life, we hear the group banging on the door, wanting to be released. At the end of the aria, the banging resumes loudly and the aria concludes with the pursuers breaking down the door.

—WILLIAM M. HOFFMAN

Slow and plodding, ♩ = ca. 68

I pant _____ when I walk. I wheeze _____ when I talk.

My mus-cles are slack. _____ I've a pain in my back. My mon — ey is

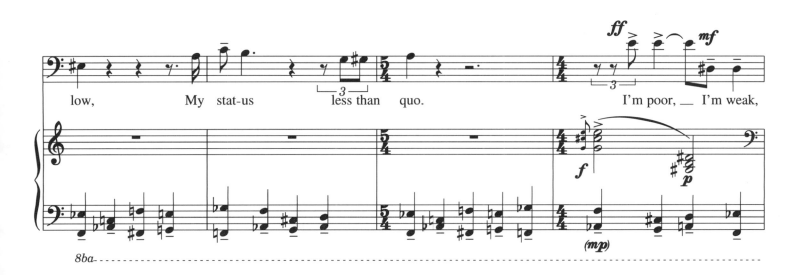

low, My stat-us less than quo. I'm poor, _ I'm weak,

4

Vet'r-in-ar-i-an, E-gal-i-tar-i-an, Heath-en co-me-di-an, Pi-ous tra-

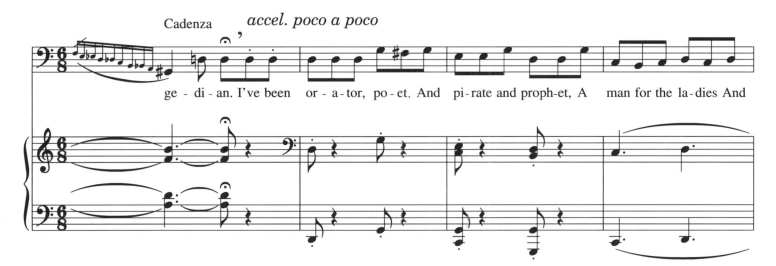

Cadenza · *accel. poco a poco*

ge-di-an. I've been or-a-tor, po-et, And pi-rate and proph-et, A man for the la-dies And

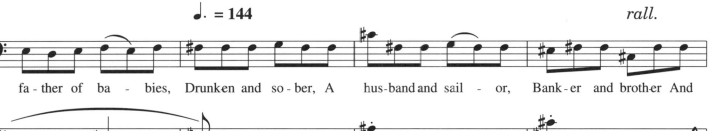

♩. = 144 · *rall.*

fa-ther of ba - bies, Drunk-en and so-ber, A hus-band and sail - or, Bank-er and broth-er And

Subito a tempo (♩. = 144)

with élan

ossia:

bar-ber and lov - er. Dip-lo-mat, ac-ro-bat, Teach-er of et - i - quette, Stu-dent and swords-man,

6

I've seen ev'ry-thing, done ev'ry-thing, had ev'ry-thing,

and lost ev'-ry-thing. _____ Of what then are they jea-lous? _____

lightly tremolo to keep
sounding (add sost. ped.)

My spir - it: _____ A _____ va - por del-

- li - ques - cent, _____ An ef - fer - ves - cent liq - uid Per - vad-ing, in - va -

ding, tak-ing my bod - y, Mak-ing me flu - id, light, _ buoy-ant. I'm sun-light, a

moon-beam, And care-free I fly to the stars. Ca-pel - la, Ca-ri - na,

Spi - ca, Au-ri - ga, Li - bra, Ly - ra. An - dro - me-da, For - nax,

Phoe-nix, Bell - a - trix, Pol - lux. Joy! _____ Joy! _____ Care - free I

* Throughout this section, this chord should be held with the sostenuto pedal. Every
2 or 3 measures, trill on a chord tone or play a soft arpeggio to keep the sound going.

fly to the stars: _____ Vul - pec - u - la, Ve - la, Co -

(as before)

mp

(as before)

(as before)

lum - ba, A - ra, La - cer - ta, Lu - pus, Le - pus. Joy! _____

(trem.) *(non trem.)*

sf *mp*

Joy! _____ Joy! _____ Peg - a - sus, Per - se - us, A - qui - la.

♩. = 144

p *mp* *mf*

mp *mf*

mf

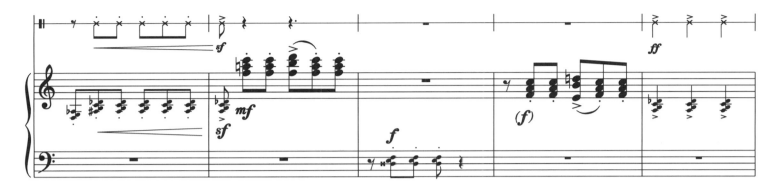

They wish they could kill me.

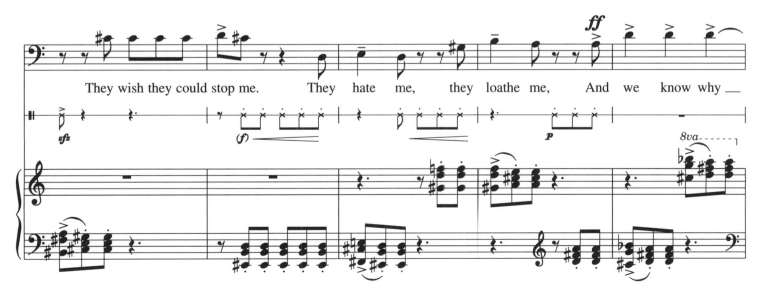

They wish they could stop me. They hate me, they loathe me, And we know why ___

they must tor-ment me so!

They're

jeal - ous!

They're jeal - ous!

They're jeal-ous they're jeal - ous.

They're jeal - - - - ous!

Yes,

jeal - - - - ous–

Of

Fig - -

- -a - ro, _____ your Fig - a - ro.

ff

add octaves when possible

I'm back at last! _____ I've been a vet-er-i-nar-i-an,

ossia:

E-gal-i-tar-i- an, Heath-en co -me- di - an, Pi-ous tra - ge-di - an, Or-a-tor, po-et, And pir-ate and prop-het, A

poco rall.

man for the la-dies And fath-er of ba - bies, Drunk-en and so-ber, A hus-band and sail - or, Bank-er and broth-er And

A tempo

bar - ber and lov - er. Dip - lo - mat, ac - ro - bat, Teach-er of et - i - quette, me!

Sat - ir - ist, pes - sim-ist, Sur - geon and Cal - vin - ist, I've

been dip - lo - mat, ac - ro - bat, Teach - er of et - i - quette, Stu - dent and swords - man,

ossia: si - cian,

Spy and mu - si - cian, Sat - ir - ist, pes - sim-ist, Sur-geon and Cal - vin - ist, Span - ish e - con - o - mist,